WILD EARTH

EARTHQUAKES!

BY RENÉE GRAY-WILBURN

ILLUSTRATED BY ALEKSANDAR SOTIROVSKI

Consultant: Susan L. Cutter, PhD
Director, Hazards and Vulnerability Research Institute
Department of Geography
University of South Carolina
Columbia, South Carolina

CAPSTONE PRESS
a capstone imprint

First Graphics are published by Capstone Press,
1710 Roe Crest Drive, North Mankato, Minnesota 56003.
www.capstonepub.com

Library of Congress Cataloging-in-Publication Data
Gray-Wilburn, Renée.
  Earthquakes! / by Renée Gray-Wilburn ; illustrated by Aleksander
Sotirovski.
      p. cm.—(First graphics. wild earth)
  Includes bibliographical references and index.
  Summary: "In graphic novel format, text and illustrations explain how
earthquakes happen, how their strength is measured, and how to stay safe
during one"—Provided by publisher.
  ISBN 978-1-4296-7605-2 (library binding)
  ISBN 978-1-4296-7950-3 (paperback)
  1. Earthquakes—Juvenile literature. I. Sotirovski, Aleksandar, ill. II. Title. III.
Series.
  QE521.3.G727 2012
  551.22—dc23   2011028740

Editorial Credits
Christopher Harbo, editor; Juliette Peters, designer;
    Nathan Gassman, art director; Kathy McColley,
    production specialist

Printed in the United States of America in North Mankato, Minnesota.
102016   010070R

Table of Contents

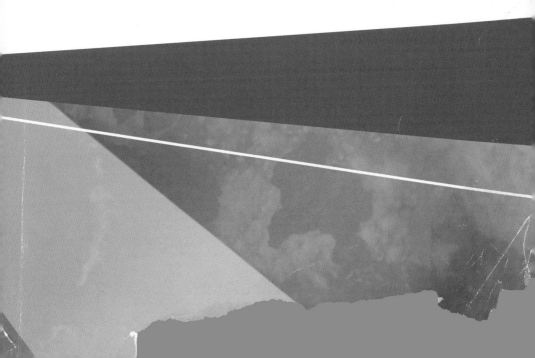

What Is an Earthquake?

It's dinnertime. Suddenly the house starts shaking.

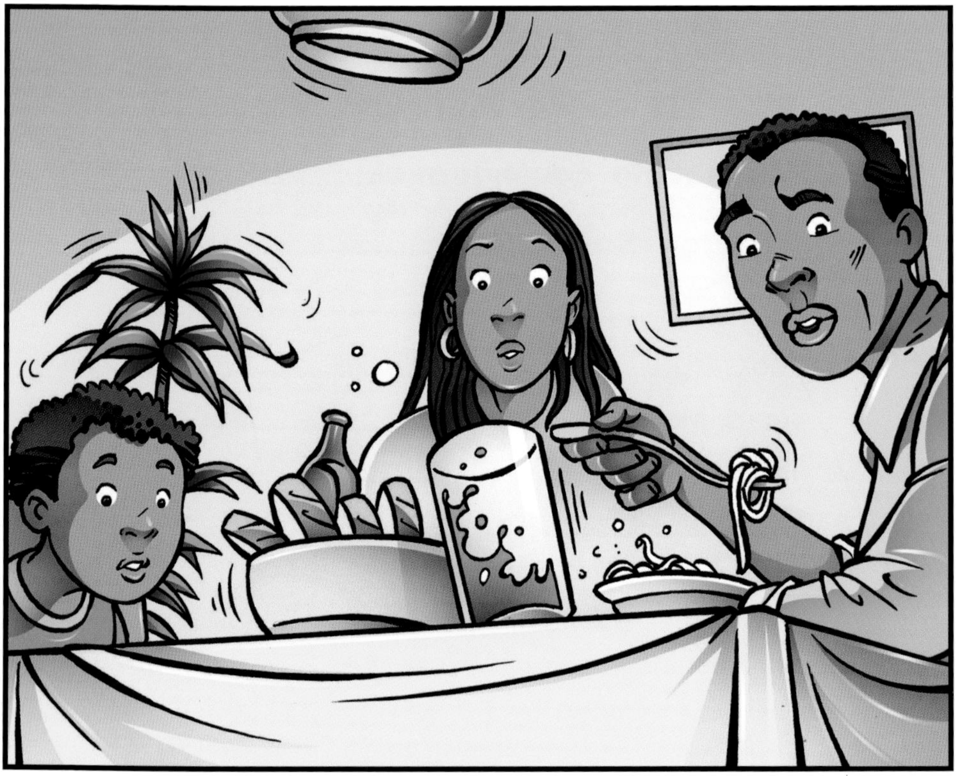

A rumbling sound fills the air.

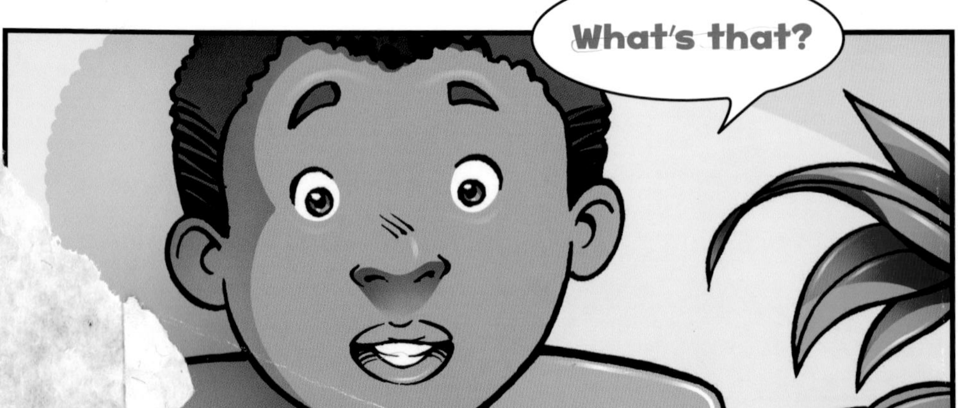
What's that?

Pictures rattle against the walls.

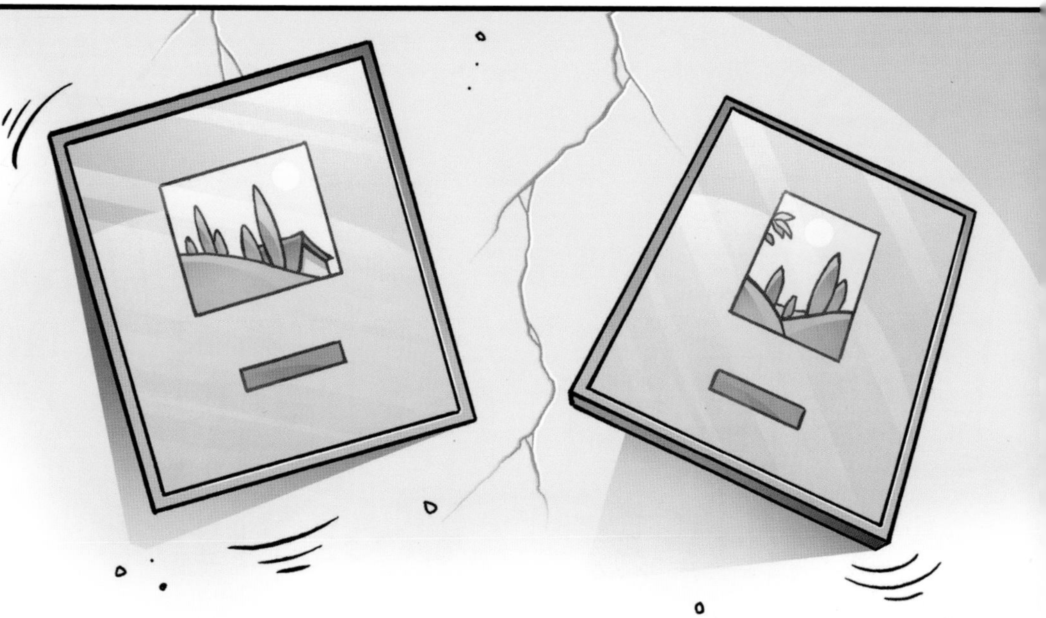

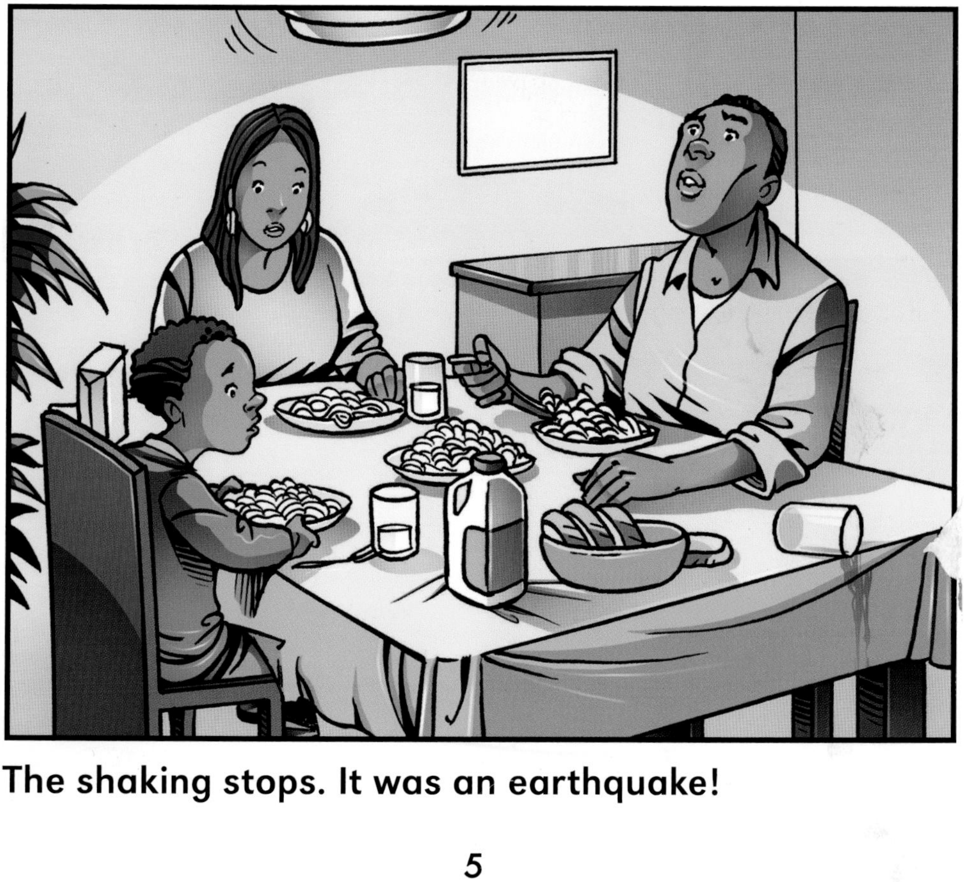

The shaking stops. It was an earthquake!

Earthquakes are sudden movements of Earth's surface.

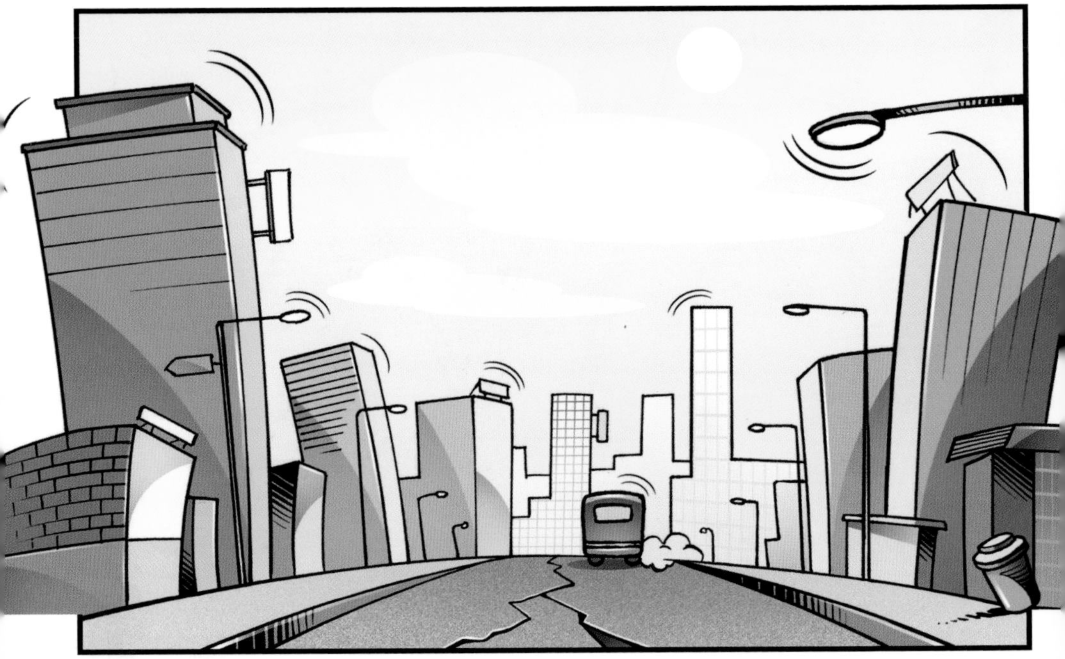

They happen when Earth's crust moves.

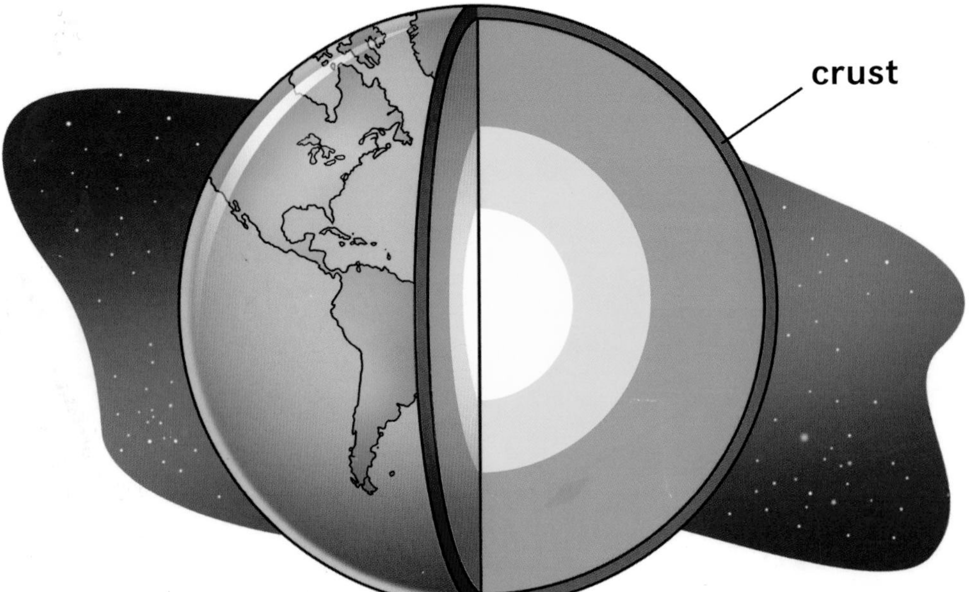
crust

Earth's crust is broken into large pieces called plates.

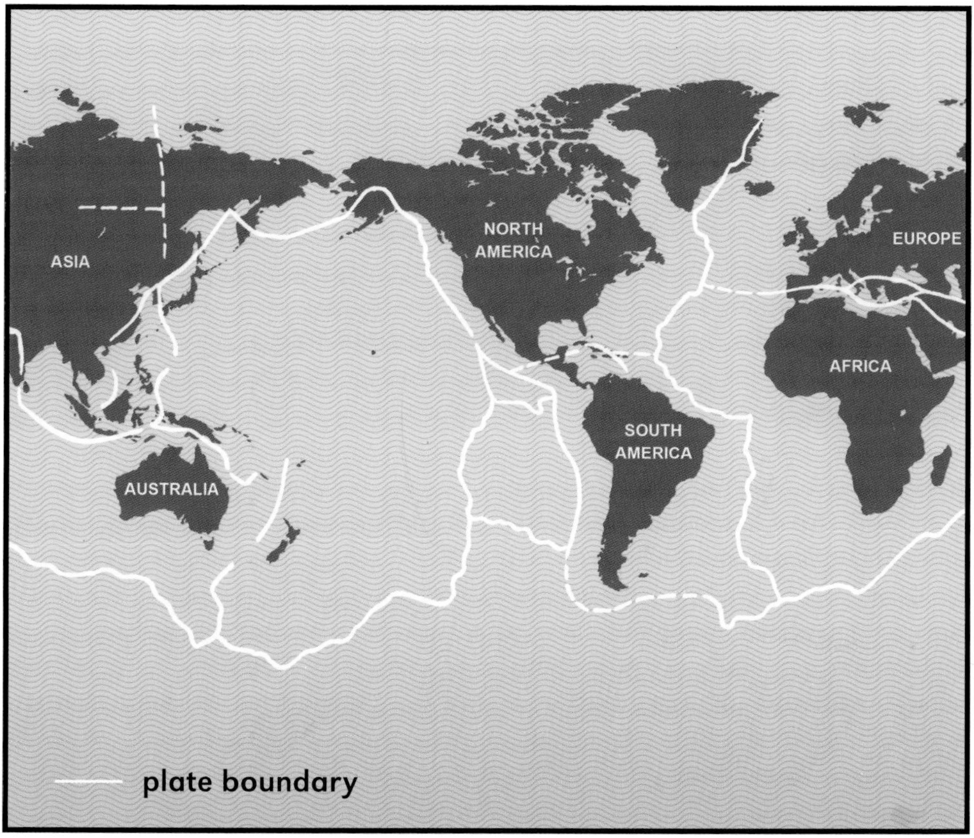
ASIA
NORTH AMERICA
EUROPE
AFRICA
SOUTH AMERICA
AUSTRALIA
plate boundary

Earth's plates move slowly. Plates push against each other at places called faults.

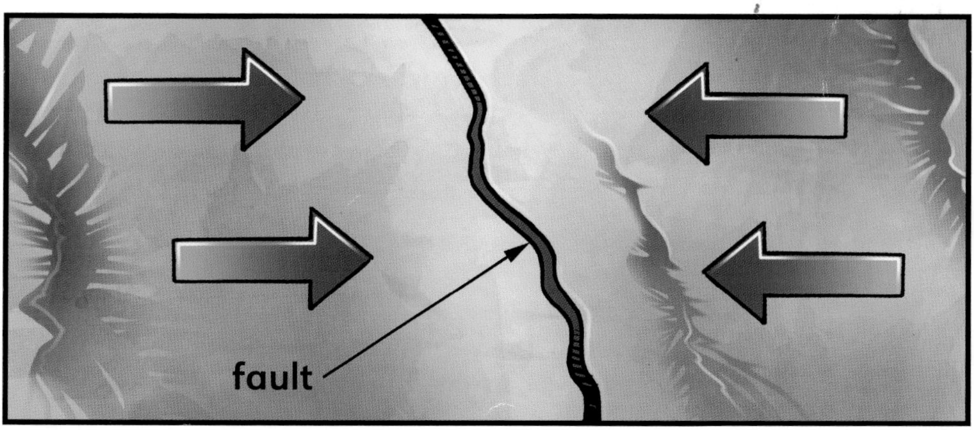
fault

As plates move, energy is released. This energy causes earthquakes along the fault line.

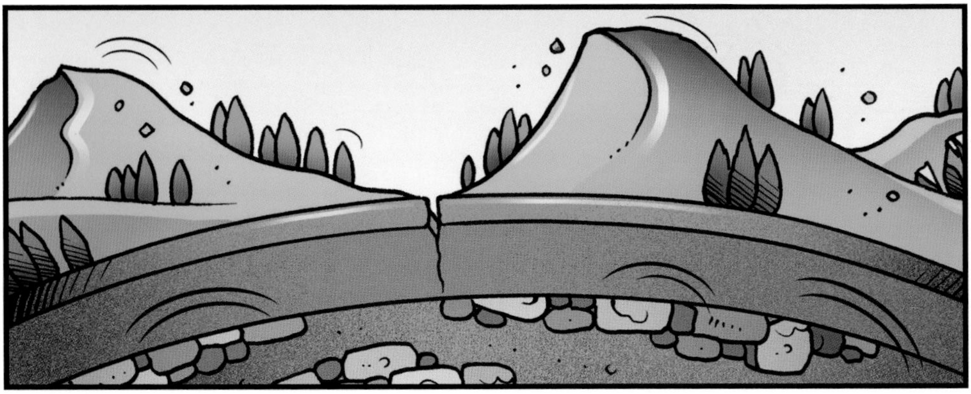

Forces sometimes cause one side of the fault to rise. The other side falls.

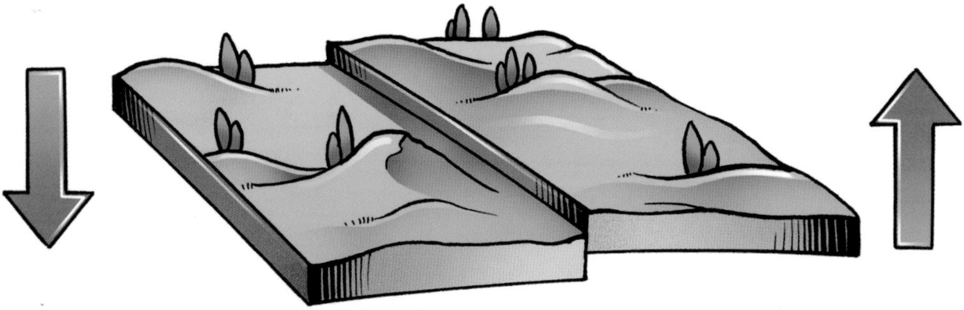

Other times the two sides of the fault slide past each other.

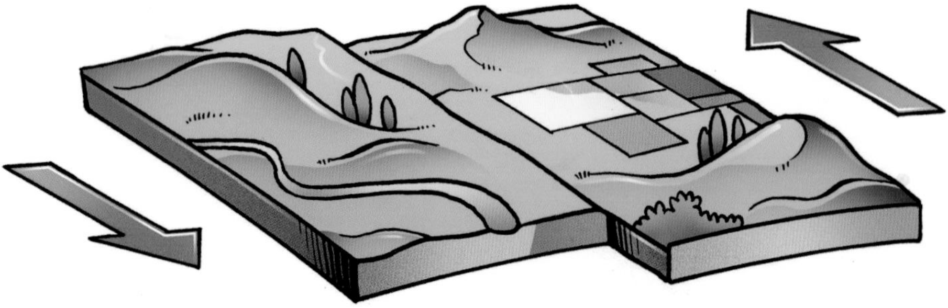

Earthquakes can happen anywhere a fault lies.

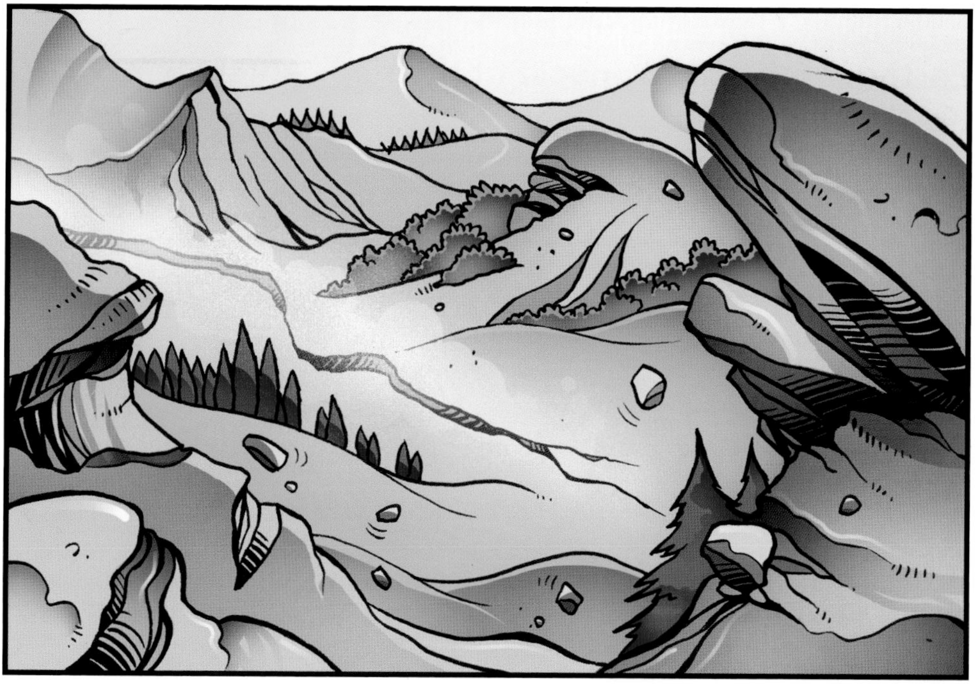

But most happen along the Ring of Fire.

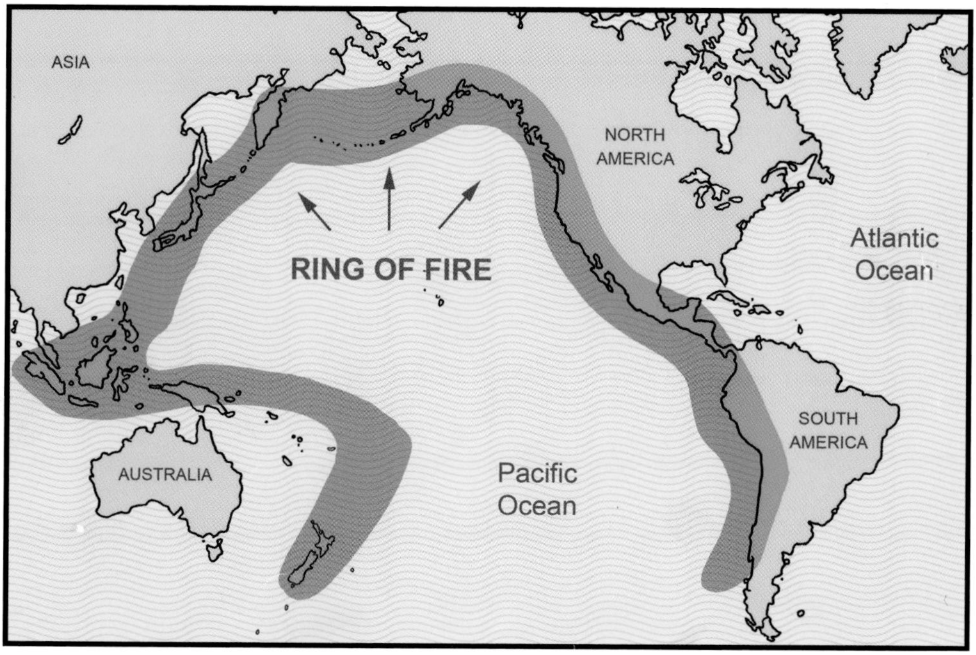
ASIA
NORTH AMERICA
RING OF FIRE
Atlantic Ocean
SOUTH AMERICA
AUSTRALIA
Pacific Ocean

Measuring Earthquakes

Earthquakes are strongest at their epicenter. This spot on Earth's surface is directly above where an earthquake began.

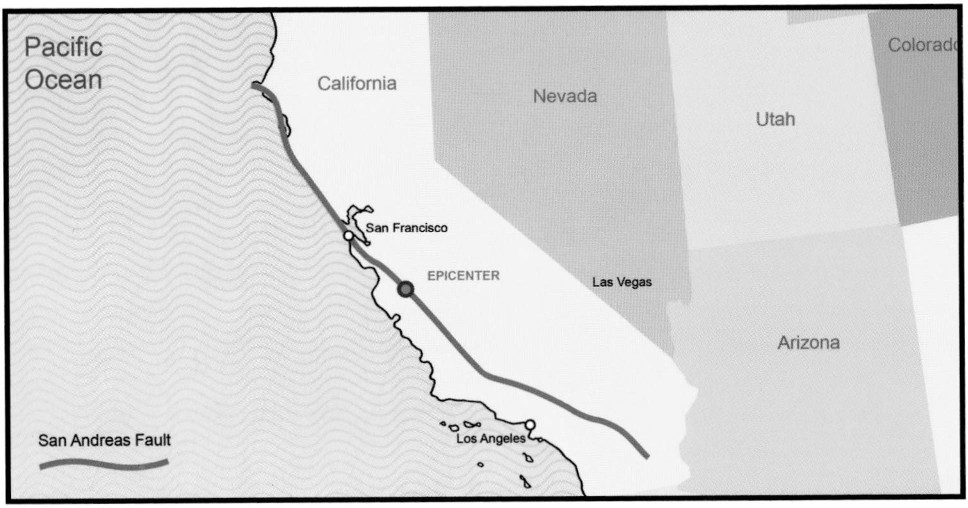

Pacific Ocean
California
Nevada
Utah
Colorado
San Francisco
EPICENTER
Las Vegas
Arizona
Los Angeles
San Andreas Fault

Seismic waves travel in circles away from the epicenter.

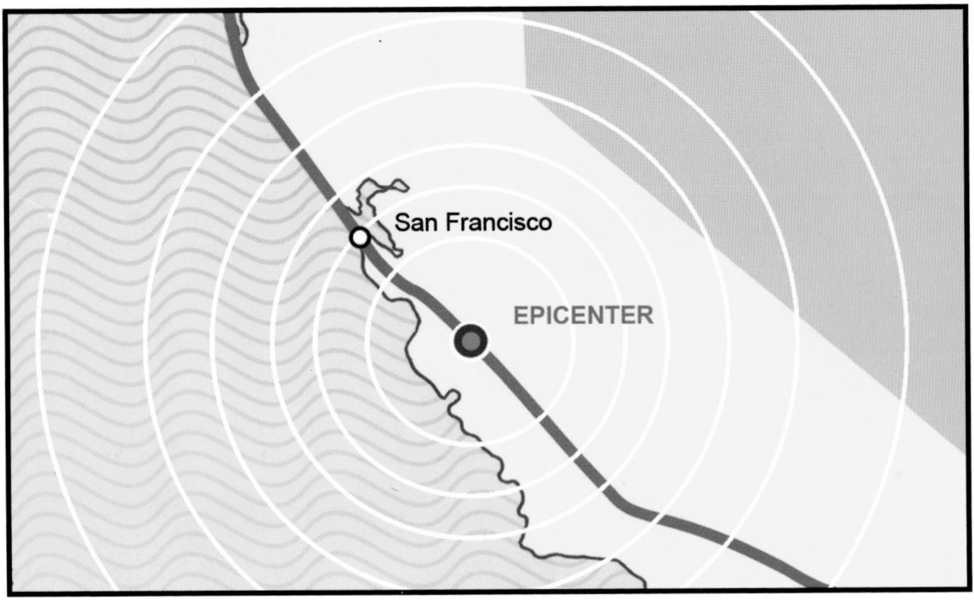

San Francisco
EPICENTER

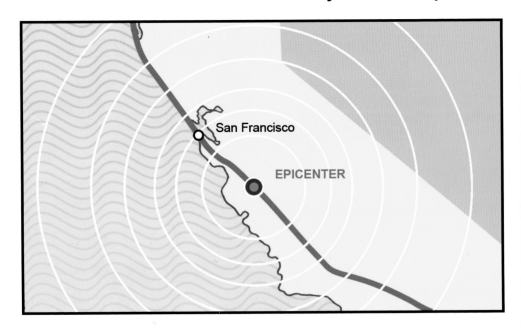

These waves can shake the ground for hundreds of miles.

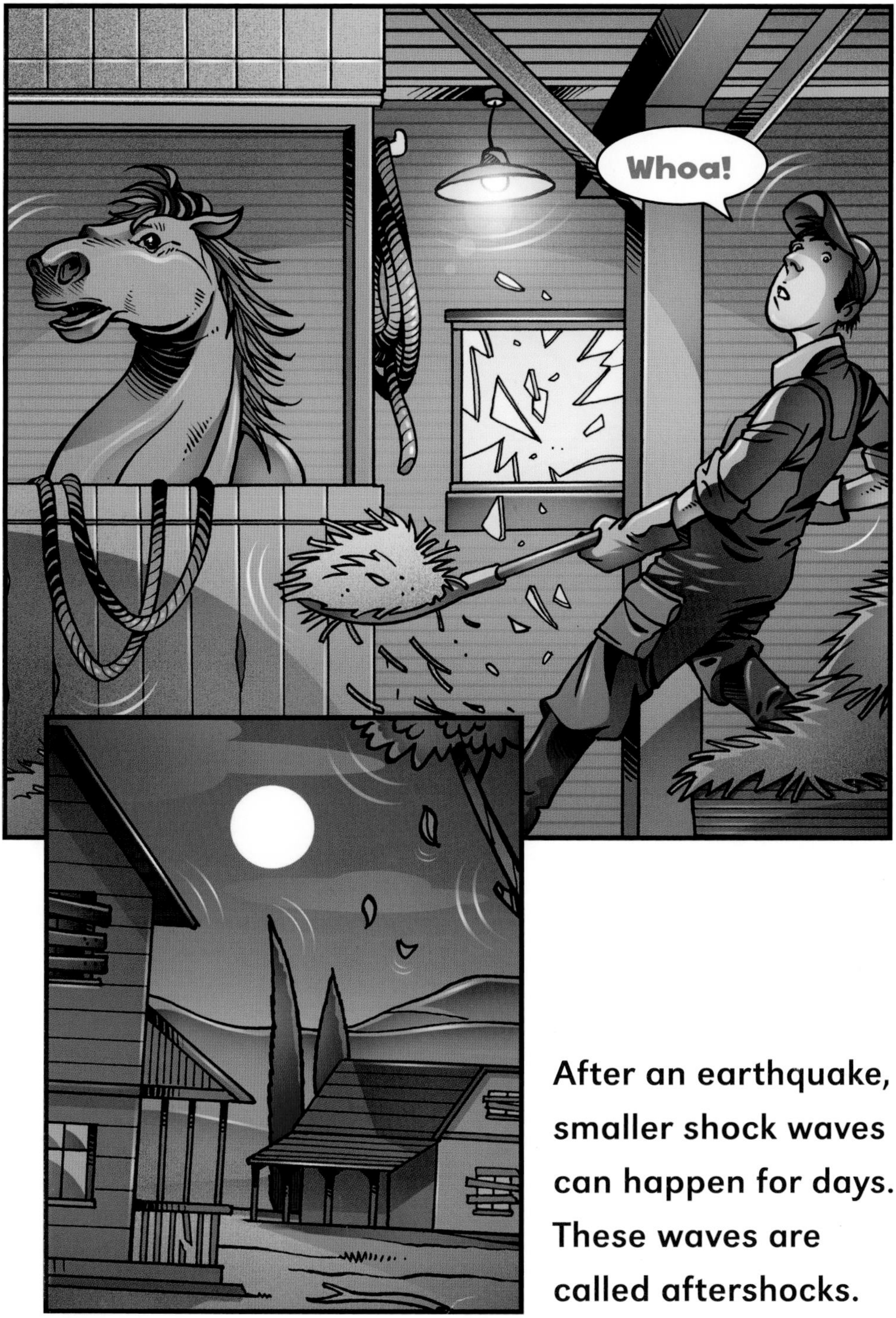
Whoa!

After an earthquake, smaller shock waves can happen for days. These waves are called aftershocks.

Scientists use the Richter scale to measure seismic waves.

This scale rates an earthquake's power from zero to 10.

Richter Scale	
0 - 2	can't feel
3 - 4	no damage
5	some damage
6	much damage
7	severe damage
8 - 10	possible total ruin

Most earthquakes are under 3.0.

They are too small to feel.

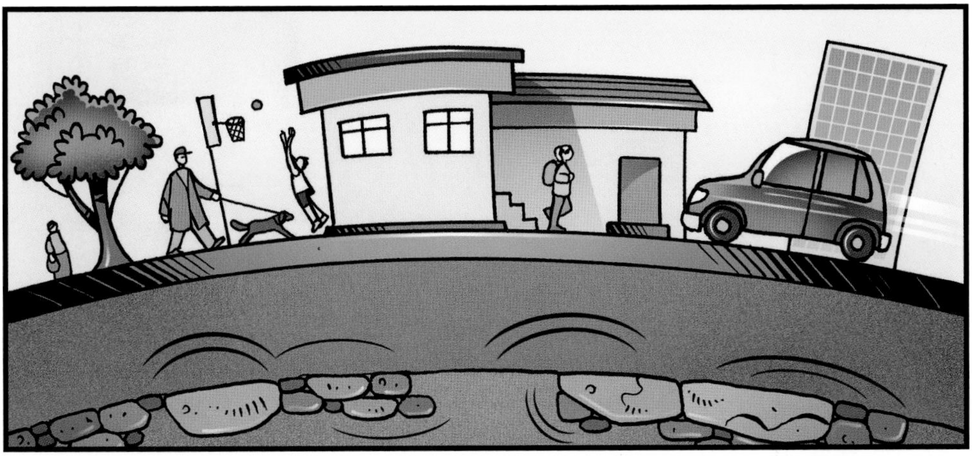

But strong earthquakes above 5.0 cause damage.

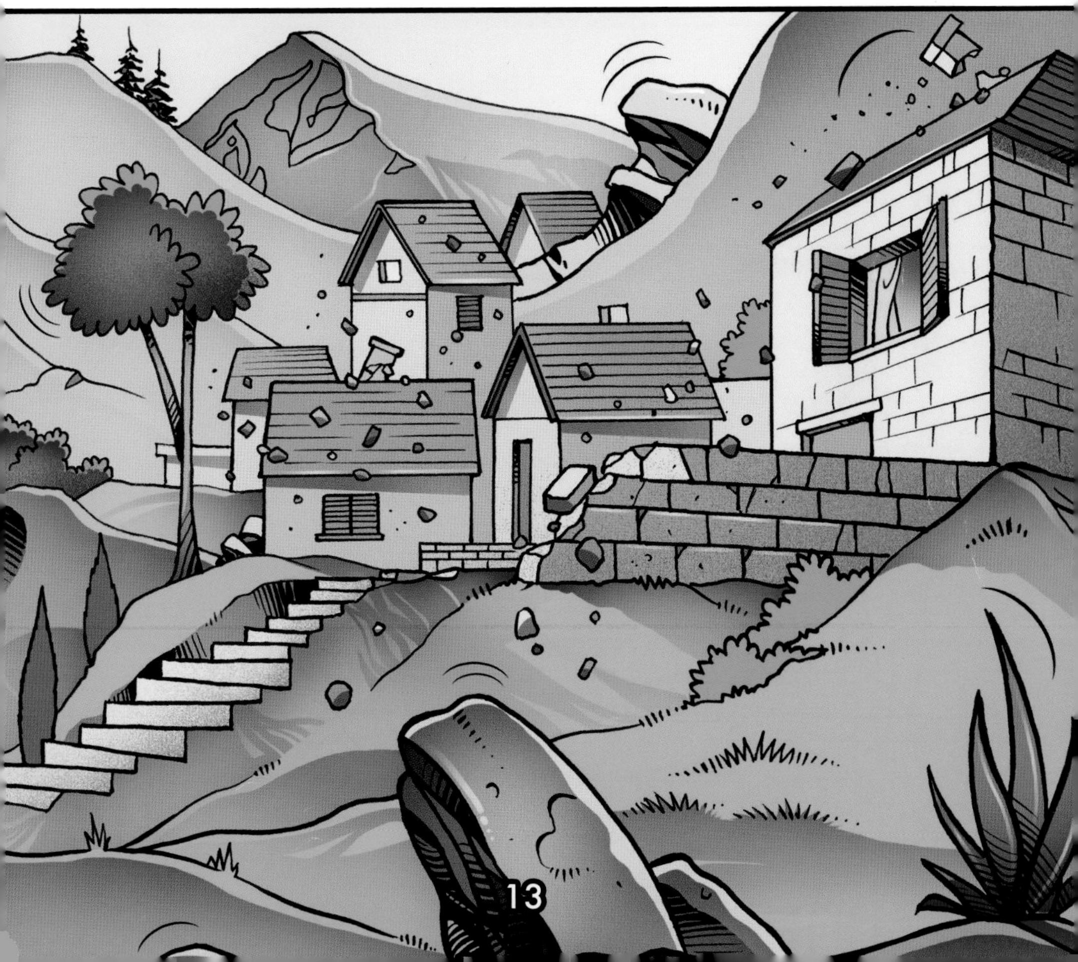

Strong earthquakes can crumble buildings and break bridges.

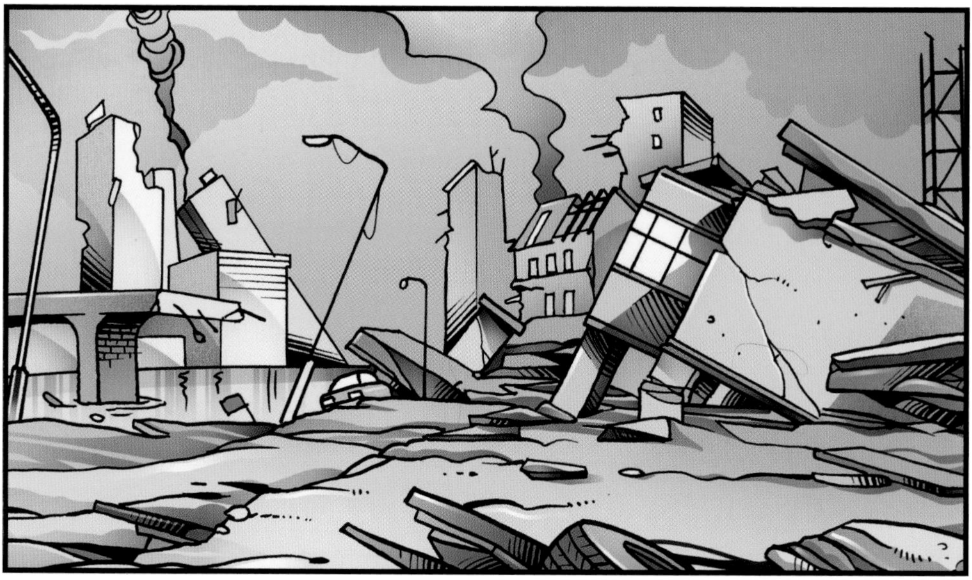

Earthquakes can break water lines. Broken lines mean there is no water to put out fires. Buildings often burn down after earthquakes.

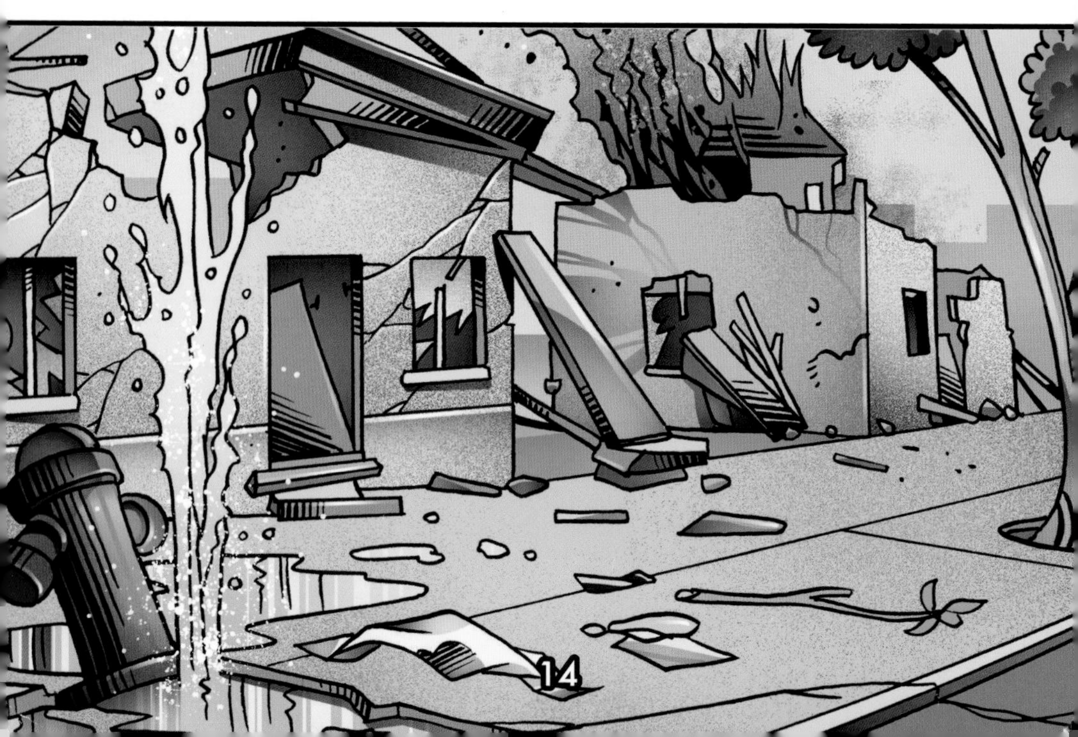

Earthquakes send rocks, dirt, and snow tumbling down hills and mountains.

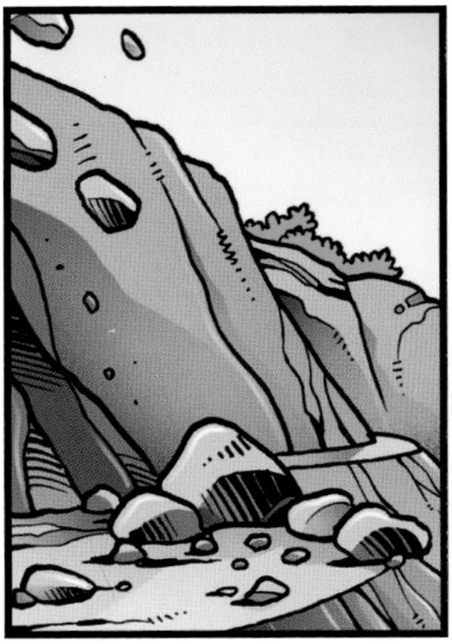

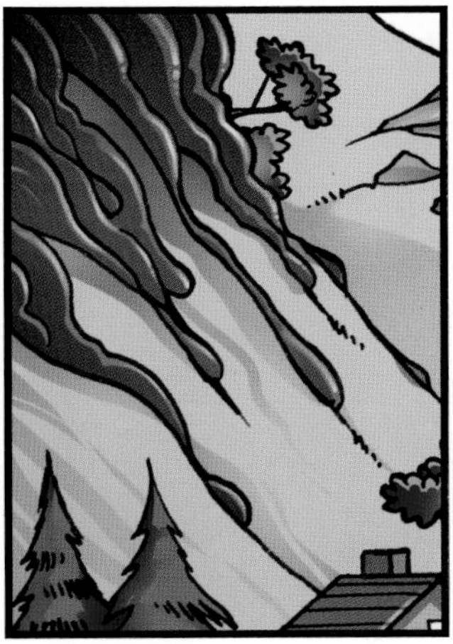

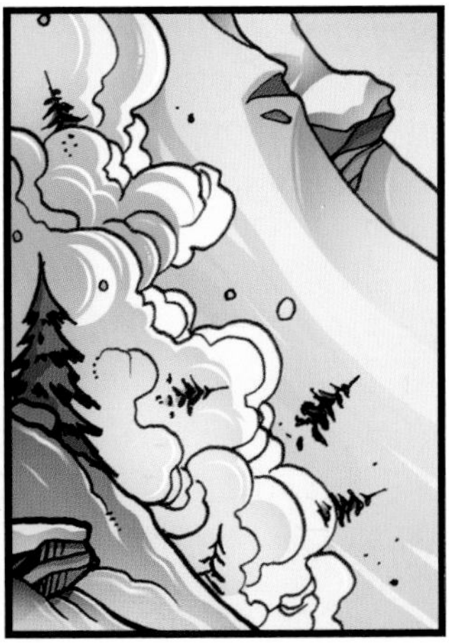

Underwater earthquakes cause the ocean to move. Large waves called tsunamis can destroy whole towns.

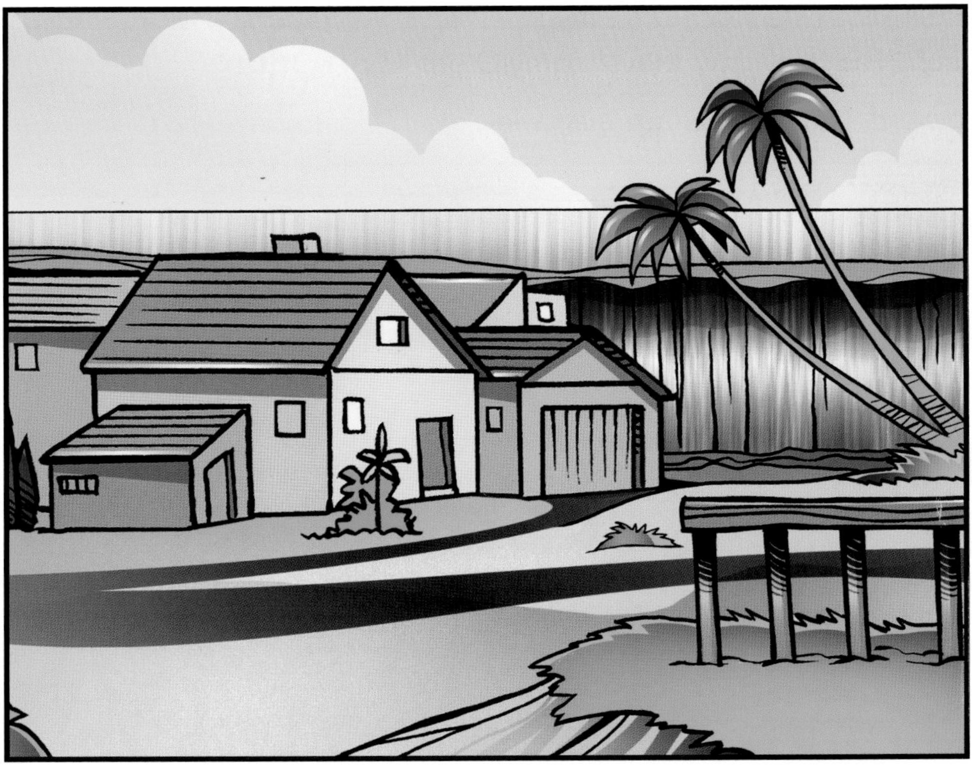

Staying Safe

No one knows when or where earthquakes will happen.

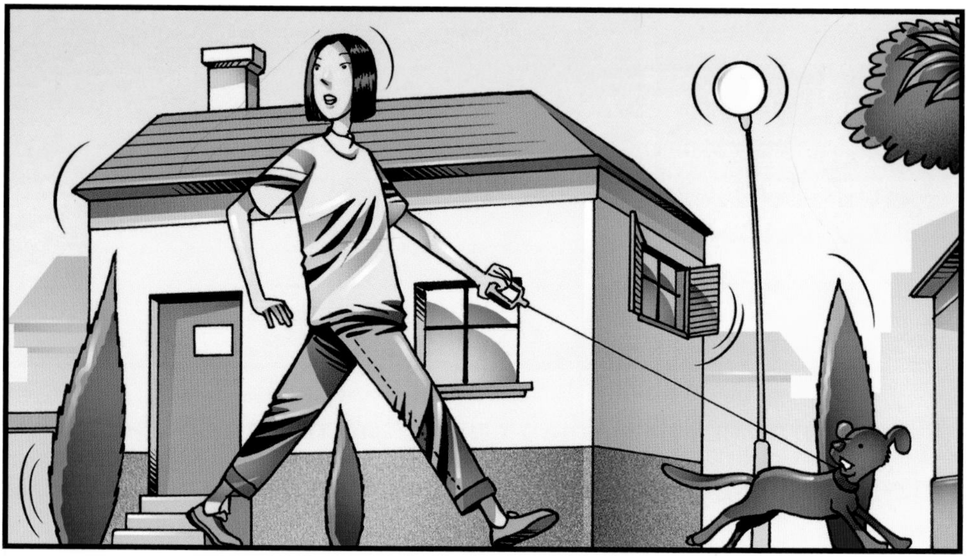

Scientists study earthquakes to learn more about them.

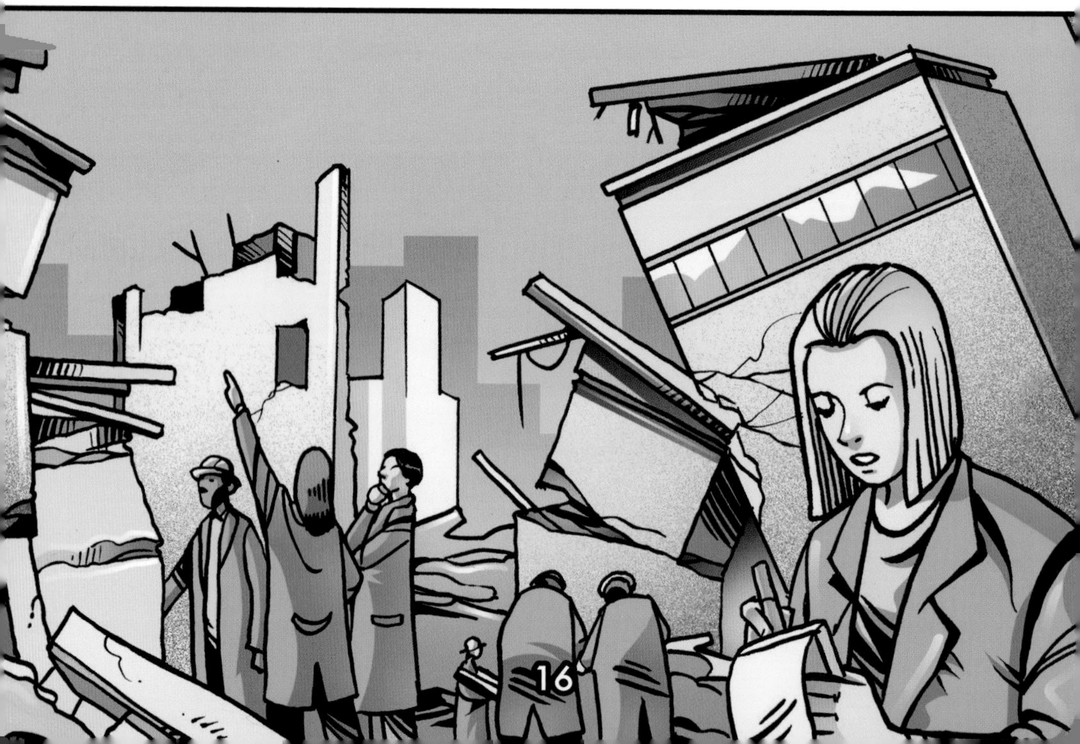

They study faults to understand how Earth's plates move.

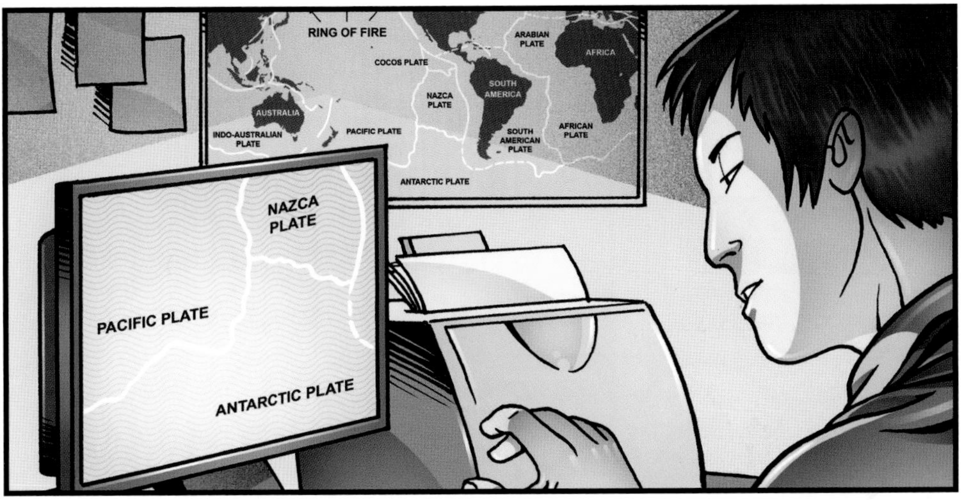
RING OF FIRE
COCOS PLATE
ARABIAN PLATE
AFRICA
SOUTH AMERICA
NAZCA PLATE
AUSTRALIA
INDO-AUSTRALIAN PLATE
PACIFIC PLATE
SOUTH AMERICAN PLATE
AFRICAN PLATE
ANTARCTIC PLATE
NAZCA PLATE
PACIFIC PLATE
ANTARCTIC PLATE

Scientists share what they learn to help people prepare for earthquakes.

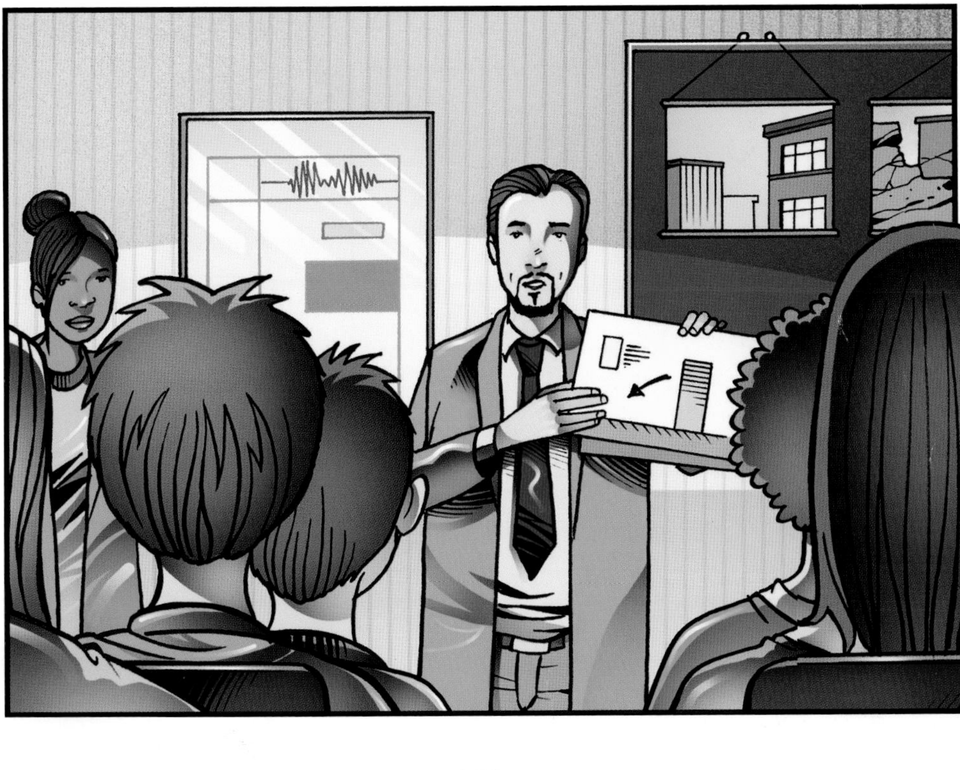

Builders use information about earthquakes.

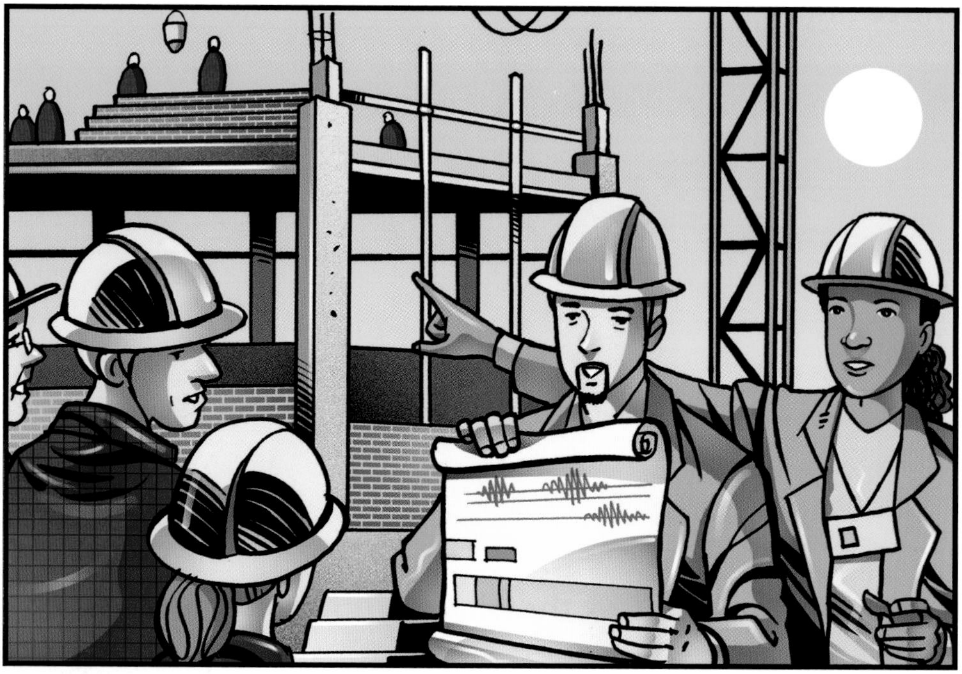

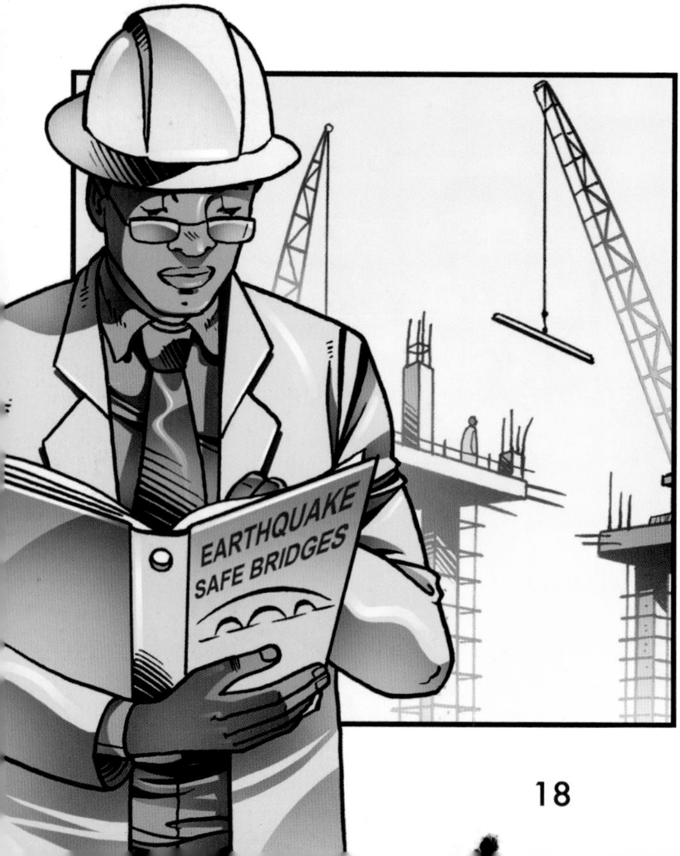
EARTHQUAKE
SAFE BRIDGES

They try to make bridges and buildings that can stand up to earthquakes.

Buildings made of brick crumble when they shake. Builders make stronger buildings by using steel.

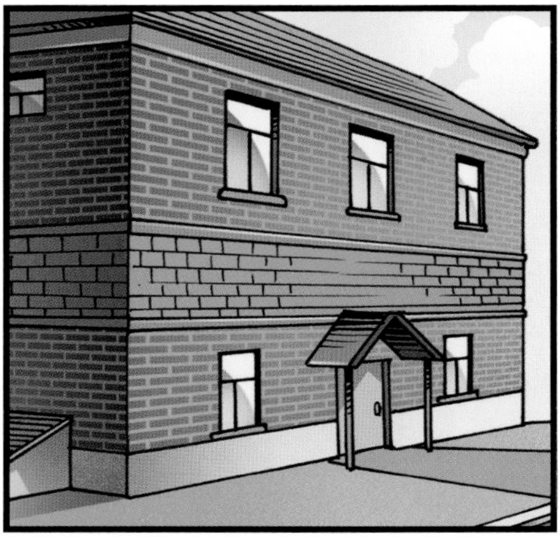

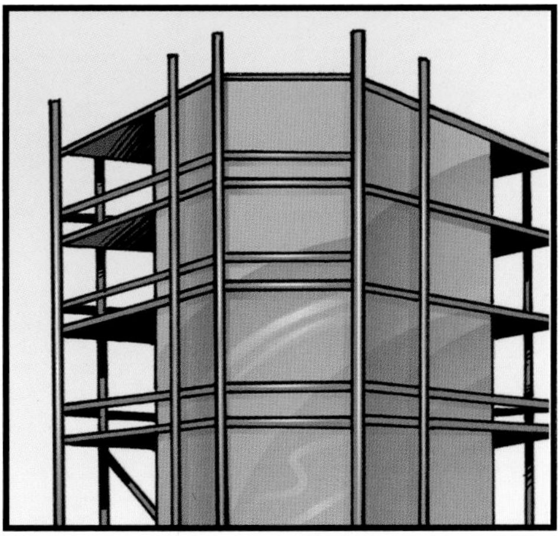

When buildings shake, steel helps them bend, but not break.

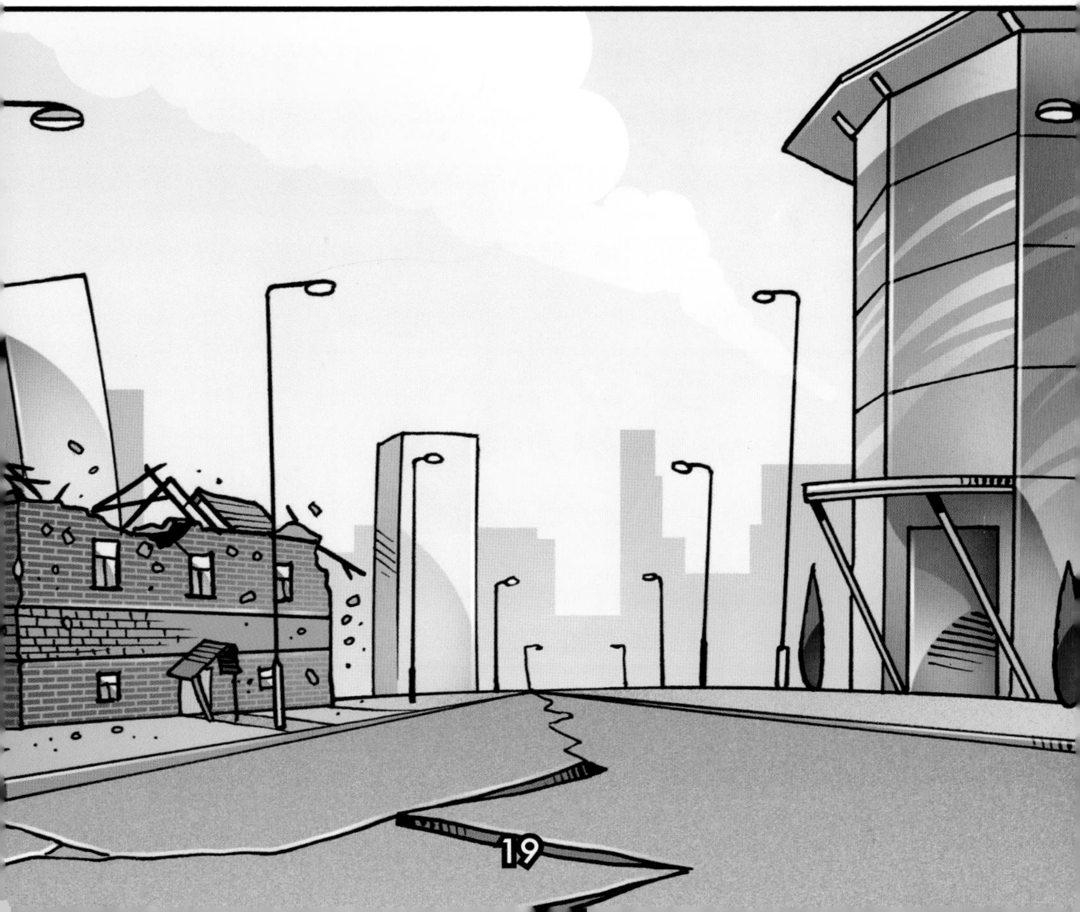

You never know when an earthquake will happen. But you can learn what to do when one strikes.

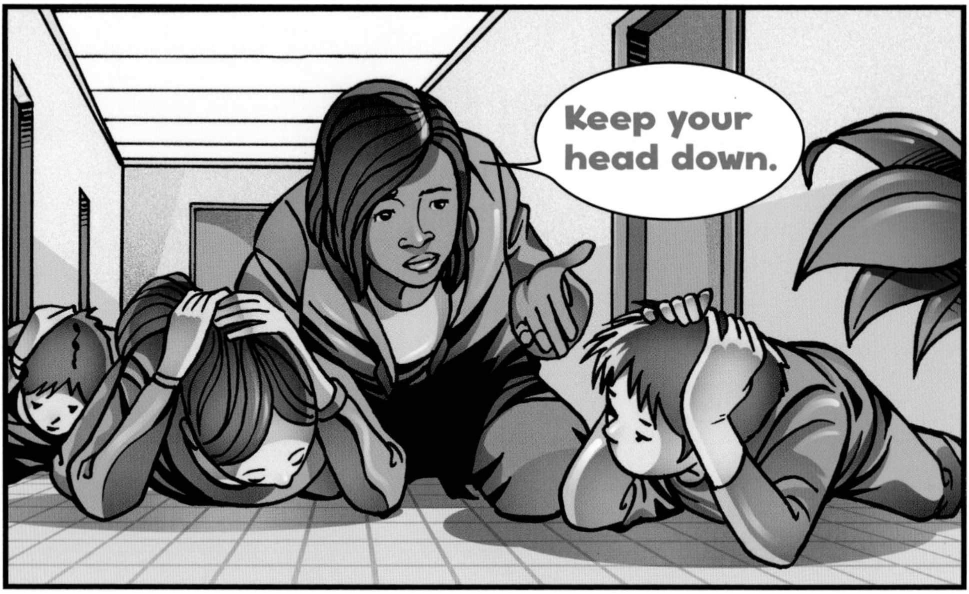
Keep your head down.

If you're inside, stay there. Hide under a table, and cover your head.

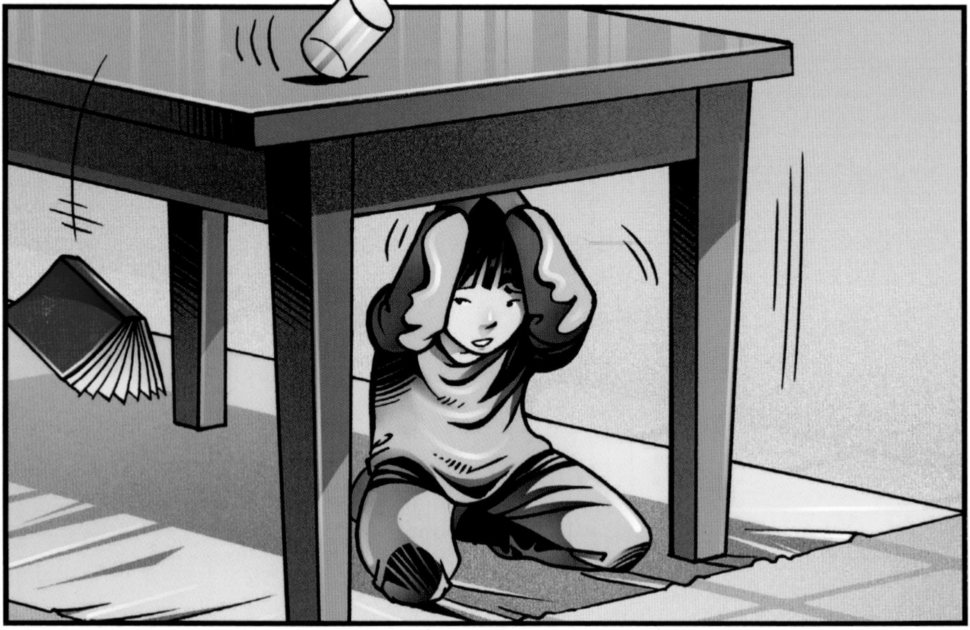

If you're outside, drop to the ground. Keep away from buildings, trees, or anything that might fall.

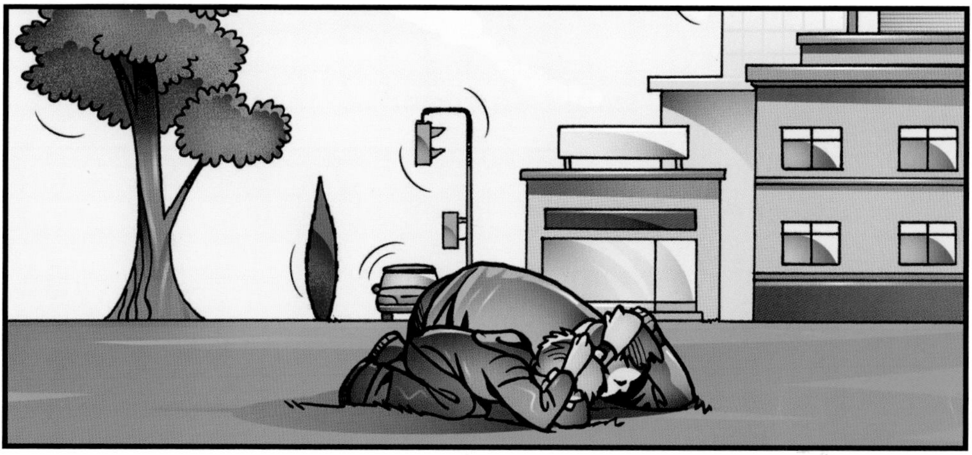

Knowing what to do during an earthquake helps keep you safe.

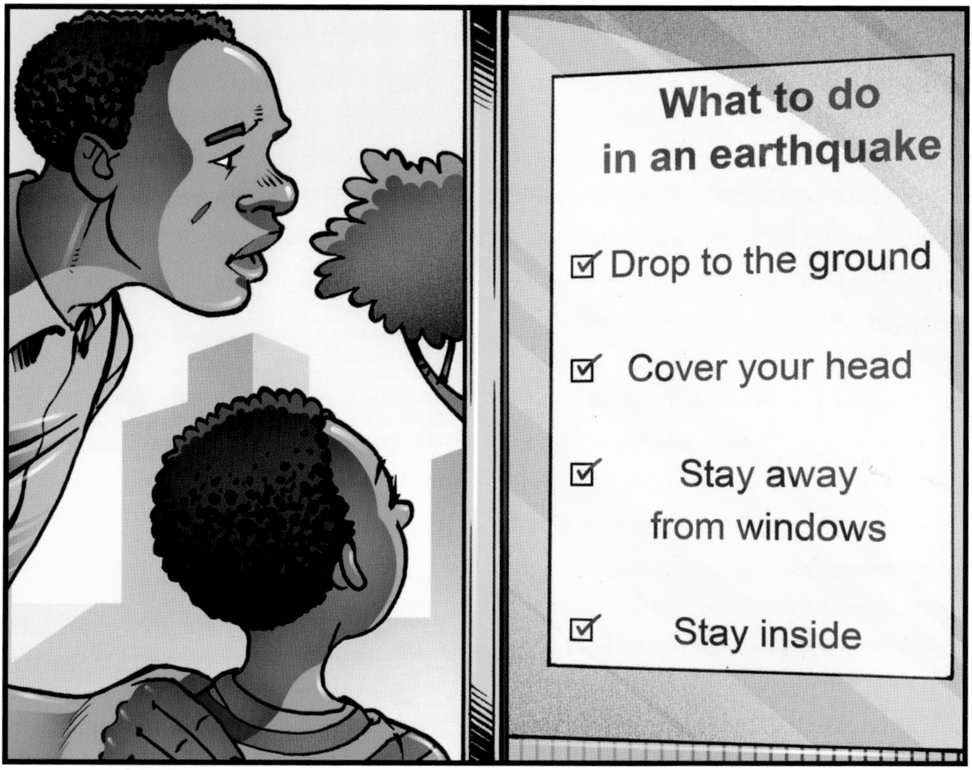
What to do
in an earthquake
Drop to the ground
Cover your head
Stay away from windows
Stay inside

Glossary

aftershock—a small earthquake that follows a larger one

crust—the hard outer layer of Earth

epicenter—the spot on Earth's surface directly above where an earthquake begins

fault—a crack in Earth's crust where rocks on either side move past each other

plate—a large sheet of rock that is a piece of Earth's crust

seismic waves—unseen waves in the ground created by an earthquake

tsunami—a large ocean wave caused by an underwater earthquake

Read More

Bauer, Marion Dane. *Earthquake!* Ready-to-Read. New York: Aladdin, 2009.

Mara, Wil. *How Do Earthquakes Happen?* Tell Me Why, Tell Me How. New York: Marshall Cavendish Benchmark, 2011.

Schuh, Mari C. *Earthquakes*. Earth in Action. Mankato, Minn.: Capstone Press, 2010.

Internet Sites

FactHound offers a safe, fun way to find Internet sites related to this book. All of the sites on FactHound have been researched by our staff.

Here's all you do:

Visit *www.facthound.com*

Type in this code: 9781429676052

Check out projects, games and lots more at
www.capstonekids.com

23

Index

WILD EARTH

Titles in this Set:

EARTHQUAKES!

HURRICANES!

TORNADOES!

VOLCANOES!

FIRST GRAPHICS